This is a work of fiction. Names, characters, places, and incidents either are the product of the author's imagination or are used fictitiously. Any resemblance to actual persons, living or dead, events, or locales is entirely coincidental.

© Copyright by Fantastic Fables

All rights reserved. No part of this book may be reproduced or used in any manner without written permission of the copyright owner except for the use of quotations in a book review.

A Rebellion Rabbit rivals a Mighty Lion
ISBN 978-1-990544-77-4 (Hardcover)
ISBN 978-1-990544-82-8 (Paperback)
ISBN 978-1-990544-07-1 (Ebook)

A Fantastic Fables Publication

There was a dense forest full of wild animals. The forest was thick enough that some parts were in the dark, even in the daylight. All animals, from small to large, lived and hunted in the same jungle but were all afraid of one fierce lion. A lion whose roar shambled even the biggest of them. When he roamed in the morning for food, even the most ferocious of them looked for a hideout. He took whatever he wished for that day. No one even dared to counter his will.

But one day, after the lion left with his prey, the fox stood on a high rock and said, "Come out! Oh, animals of this forest. Come out and listen to my advice!"

The fox had a reputation for being clever amongst the animals. So they came near and gathered around. "What is it now? I am in no mood to listen to anyone's nonsense talk. The lion took my son away," the deer started sobbing.

"Yes, this fox is very cunning. He will surely say something to deceive us and benefit himself. He only uses others," the turtle added. He was the best friend of the deer and was very upset about his friend's loss.

"You were not here last night, my brother. You don't know how we all had to save ourselves last night," the ox was talking to the antelope, who was out of the jungle the night before.

The bear said, "Yesss, he's right! Thank God! Last night, I found a big and dense tree and climbed it to hide from the lion."

"And I was lucky enough to find a secret hole in a rock and saved my family. That's why I am alive today," the rabbit added.

Slowly, all the animals gathered and started sharing their survival tactics, ignoring the fox. The fox became frustrated and shouted, "Shut up, you fools, and listen to me. It is our lives at stake here. How long can you survive this lion? You all know how powerful his sight is. He knows all the forest. All your hideaways will be found by him one way or another."

"So, what are we going to do? Fight him? You are suggesting that we should fight him," the deer said angrily. "I have lost my son. What could I do except for watching miserably and listening to his painful screams from a distance? I definitely couldn't afford to fight him. Could I? He is a lot more powerful than any of us and even if I try to fight him, not only will I fail, but he'll also eat the rest of my children!" The deer screamed and then broke down into tears.

"Yes, she is right. We cannot fight him. Who dares to go to his den? It's the law of the jungle. The powerful will survive, and the weak will be hunted. Haven't you heard about the survival of the fittest? Huh?" the monkey said sarcastically. "Thank you, God, for giving me the ability to climb tall trees. Thanks a lot." He teased others. Animals ignored him as always.

"Can't you guys please listen to me? I am frustrated by his fearful roar every day. Half of our day goes to waste hiding from him, and sometimes we have to go to sleep hungry at night. I am thinking of a deal with the lion," the fox said.

"What deal?" the rhino said in a hurry.

"Easy, horn head. What I am about to tell you, you all have to listen to it carefully," the fox said. "Why don't we offer him ourselves daily at his den, so we can live our day without his fear of coming? We could hunt and feed our family freely. We all know that he is going to get us one day."

The animals became furious, listening to the fox's deal.

"Are you crazy? Why would we offer ourselves if we can survive by hiding?" the bear said. "The fox thinks he is the only brainy one here. I am not going to give myself to him! I will fight if he hunts me."

"You think you are so smart? Go ahead and fight him then," the fox angrily said to the bear. He turned around to face the other animals and said, "I urge the rest of you all to think on this deal tonight and tell me your decision tomorrow after the lion's hunt."

The animals left gossiping about the foolish deal. Nobody was convinced.

The deer went to her house, which was under a big tree. She lived with her four children under that tree and grazed near it in the day. The lion ate one of her children today. The rest of her three children ran towards her the moment they saw her. They were shivering with fear and hiding behind the bushes, waiting for their mother. "Mother! Mother! Where were you?" They started crying.

She hugged them. "It's okay, my children. Don't be scared. I am here," she said to them, swallowing the lump of tears in her throat. She had to act strong in front of her innocent babies.

"Where did the lion take our brother? Will he take us too? I don't want to go with him, mother!" one of them said.

"I will not go out to graze from tomorrow. I am scared he can come any time," the other one added.

"No, my children. Don't be scared. He won't come here now. Go to sleep," she pulled them close, giving them false hope. *Maybe the fox was right. If we make this deal, at least we and our children will not have to live with this fear every second*, she thought to herself while shutting her eyes.

Then the next day came. The fierce lion entered the forest and smelled the scent of the bear. As he saw the bear hiding in the tree, he roared, standing below it. The entire forest trembled, and the air stopped blowing. In the deadly silence, the animals hiding nearby heard the echo of his roar.

The lion clutched the big bear's foot in a single jump and dragged him down. By then, the bear was ready to fight back. Then they both roared furiously and muscled into each other. After a lot of punching, scratching, and throwing each other away multiple times, the lion's powerful claws mauled the bear and left him lifeless. The bear's strength paled in front of the lion. He ate and dragged the remaining body to his den.

The animals were out now with fear and hopelessness. The deer had already convinced her best friend, the turtle, to accept the deal the fox had suggested. And so, they both talked to the rest of the animals of the jungle.

"My friends, you have already seen the end of the bear who thought he could fight the lion. We are left with no other options but to make this deal. Death is inevitable, but living in the fear of death isn't! Let's do this," said the turtle.

They all agreed, went to the fox and said, "We think you were right. Being rebellious or trying to win against this lion will do us no good. In fact, it will bring us more harm. We should ponder on the deal with the lion. What do we have to do now?"

In the evening, they all went to the lion's den. They were scared to talk to him. The lion was staggered to see them all.

"We... came.... to make a deal with you," the fox stuttered.

The lion stood up and raised his eyebrows.

"We want to offer one of us to you every day, of our own will. This way you don't have to come and hunt us into the jungle, and we will live and hunt all day without fear of being hunted by you," said the fox.

A long silence prevailed.

After thinking for some moments, the lion came near the fox and said with his heavy voice, "Is this some trickery or you are honest with your words today?"

The fox looked down in fear and said, "O King! Trust me, as I came with all animals of the forest."

"Hmm..." The lion climbed on a rock, thinking about it. "Alright, I accept your deal," the lion announced. "If you all remain true to your deal, I won't come to hunt. BUT!" The lion came in front of all the animals and roared, "If I smell any deception among you, then you all saw what happened to the bear today."

They all came back. They had succeeded, but at what cost? Everyone was upset. They had saved themselves from the fear of death, or had they? "What have we done? My heart is aching. I was telling you guys this was a foolish idea. Who will be the first prey? Nobody will be ready for it!" said the antelope furiously.

Now all the animals gathered around, canvassing who would become the lion's next food. The antelope was right. Nobody was ready to offer themselves first. At last, it was decided that they would draw lots, and the unlucky one had to become the lion's food.

"This is so stupid. We were afraid of death and to escape it, we fall into this new trap of the cunning fox. Earlier, we feared the lion every second. Now we will fear this stupid gathering every evening where we'll draw lots. Everyone will fear hearing their name come out on the chit. It is going to be a lot more difficult to walk to the den when we are hopeless. When the lion hunted us, at least we had hope that we might get away. This is sheer stupidity!" said an old wise zebra.

"This is no time to think of these stupid things now. You all agreed to yourselves. I did not force anyone. Now we have made the deal. You very well know what will happen if we dishonor it. Also, you are wrong! NO! We won't be living in the same fear all day. Once we see that it's not our turn today, we'll feel relaxed for the entire day until it's time to draw the lots again. Then we'll feel the fear for some time while drawing lots and again a relaxation of one whole day if our name doesn't come out. Apart from this, only one animal will live in fear, the one whose name comes out! The rest of us will live freely. Don't you see? The suffering of one but relief for the rest. It's not such a bad idea," replied the fox. She was clever, for sure. All of them agreed, and so the law was established.

Eventually, a rabbit's name was called one day. He was shaken by his imagination of getting eaten by the lion. After sunrise, he came among the animals and said, "I cannot accept this deal! How many more animals have to suffer because of this cruel lion!" the rabbit shouted.

One of the animals said, "We have made this deal with the lion in the presence of everyone. Many sacrificed their lives to honor this deal. You are not special. You have to go. He is waiting for his food."

The rabbit drowned in thought.

"Don't insult us and this deal. Go fast. Otherwise, the lion will get angry, and our lives will be at stake," the fox said.

"My friends, give me some time to think. Maybe my plan could save us all from this adversity."

"Listen, you idiot! You are merely a rabbit, so act like one. Our friends, who were more muscular than you, ended up dead. Have you forgotten the bear's demise?" the rhino said.

"It's not about the size of the body or the power of muscles. It's about using intellect and praying for God's help. He might have bestowed me with a smart plan that would save us all from the lion. What a honeybee can do, a deer can't. It's not about the size of the body. What the mind can conceive and believe, it can achieve!" the rabbit replied.

Animals were captivated by the rabbit's speech.

The fox said, "All right, rabbit. Tell us something about your plan. It must be a master plot as you plan to rival the most ferocious lion. We might be able to help you."

"It's my secret plan. I can't tell you, my friends. But I will do my best. Just pray for my success. I won't let you all down." The rabbit left, leaving them perplexed.

The rabbit came back home. His friend was waiting for him. He hugged him. He had come to bid him farewell. "I'll miss you so much, bunny. This world is so cruel as it is taking you away from me. I still remember how we both used to hop around and play in the grassy fields. We ate until our stomachs were so full that we couldn't even move. Then we used to lie down on the grass in the beautiful warm sunlight and talk for hours. Those were good days. I wish you didn't have to go. I won't be able to bear your loss." He started crying like a little infant.

The rabbit hugged him and said, "Don't worry, buddy! I have a plan. I will avenge the death of your father, who was eaten by this lion, and save us and all the rest of the animals from him too. Just pray for me." He smiled. "Wish me luck. I got to go!" They shook hands.

So, the rabbit sat for an hour, halfway to the lion's den. He was deliberately late. It was the first important step of his plan. Inside the den, the lion's blood was boiling in anger. He was furiously scratching his claws on the rock.

"I KNEW IT!... I knew that this would happen one day. They would deceive me and dishonor the deal. And now, I am famished."

The lion jumped and roared to go to the forest. But the rabbit had arrived at that exact time, having run there. Breathing heavily, he fell at the lion's feet. After catching his breath, he bowed down in front of the lion.

"Grrrr... Now you came! I was about to come to the forest and rip your skin, you betrayers!"

"I am not... we are not betrayers, my king. But I have a justification for this delay. If you allow me to speak, then I will tell you the reason. Otherwise, you can have your food," the rabbit said submissively.

"Tell me! Tell me who stopped you from coming. It will be my next meal!" the lion asked furiously.

The rabbit now played his next move, "I... I was coming on time to your den with a friend of mine. I told him to accompany me as it would be the last time we could be together. But..." he hesitated.

"Tell me faster!" the lion roared.

"But there was another lion who jumped at us. We said to him that we are the servants of a powerful lion king. He is the king of this jungle. And we are going to fulfill our deal," the rabbit said, "Then he said, 'Who is this lion? I will tear him up too.' He also held my dear friend hostage." The rabbit continued with fear, "I urge you, my king. Please come with me and teach a lesson to this lion who questions your rule on this jungle. He asked me to tell all the animals to obey him and make him their king. He wants to take over your territory, my king. This jungle belongs to you. He has trespassed your domain. You should make him your next meal at all costs, My Lord!"

The lion was hungry and furious. This clouded his thoughts. "Come with me!" He jumped and walked towards the jungle along with the rabbit. "Lead me to him, and if you are not true, I will teach you a lesson."

Now, it was time to play the last move. The rabbit led the lion through the darkest part of the jungle. The way was long, which frustrated the lion more. That was the rabbit's plan, to get the spur-of-the-moment reaction of the lion, leaving him less time to think in anger.

The rabbit stopped at some distance from a well. The well was deep but had some water. The rabbit said, "I can't go alone beyond this. The lion lives in this well and has my friend with him. My body is shaking from his fear. But if you come with me to the edge of the well, I will show you. Please come and teach this lion a lesson. Show him how mighty and powerful you are!"

"All right! I can't wait anymore! I am hungry! It's time to show my might to this lion now," the lion roared, and they both jumped to the edge of the well.

"Oh my God! There is the lion and my friend with him! **OH, I AM DEAD NOW!**" the rabbit shouted as loud as he could, pointing at the reflection of them in the water at the depth of the well.

The lion was bewildered and jumped into the well to fight the other lion. It took some time for the lion to reach the bottom of the well, as it was very deep. He had foolishly jumped upon seeing his and rabbit's reflection, and hit the rocks at the bottom. This is how he died. It was the well of his cruelty in which he deserved to fall. The rabbit's plan was a success.

The rabbit ran happily towards the forest. He entered among them shouting, "**THE LION IS DEAD!** He is gone now!'

The animals circled him, asking, "How did you do that? How can you counter the lion alone when all the other powerful animals failed?"

"I told you, it was God's help, my dear friends. He bestowed this plan on me, a small animal."

Then he told them the entire story of how he deliberately went late to the lion's den and made a story of an imaginary lion. He knew that the lion's arrogance, along with hunger, would make him frustrated, and he would jump into the well without pondering that the lion inside the well was his own reflection.

Everyone thanked the rabbit and looked at him with eyes full of gratitude. "You have avenged the death of our loved ones. We owe you. Feel free to ask for any sort of help whenever you need it. We will always be there, amigo!" said the turtle on behalf of all the other animals. They all celebrated.

Afterward, the animals lived their lives in the forest, free from the fear of the ferocious lion.

 ## Moral

The injustice of a tyrant is a dark well. The more injustice one does, the deeper is the well. Even if you're a strong lion or a giant elephant, never be cruel to others. God is with the weak when one seeks help from him. A tyrant doesn't live forever, but the curse on him abides forever!

Be kind and respectful to each other. Keep asking for God's help in bad times. And remember that the real lion is the one who constrains oneself from wrongdoings to others and helps the oppressed.

ISBN 978-1-990544-77-4 (Hardcover)
ISBN 978-1-990544-82-8 (Paperback)
ISBN 978-1-990544-07-1 (Ebook)

ISBN 978-1-990544-78-1 (Hardcover)
ISBN 978-1-990544-83-5 (Paperback)
ISBN 978-1-990544-09-5 (Ebook)

ISBN 978-1-990544-75-0 (Hardcover)
ISBN 978-1-990544-80-4 (Paperback)
ISBN 978-1-990544-03-3 (Ebook)

ISBN 978-1-990544-76-7 (Hardcover)
ISBN 978-1-990544-81-1 (Paperback)
ISBN 978-1-990544-05-7 (Ebook)

ISBN 978-1-990544-74-3 (Hardcover)
ISBN 978-1-990544-79-8 (Paperback)
ISBN 978-1-990544-01-9 (Ebook)

a Fantastic Fables Publication

www.ingramcontent.com/pod-product-compliance
Lightning Source LLC
Chambersburg PA
CBHW061350010526
44107CB00011B/894